THE
MODERN
WORLD

THE LAST
HUNDRED YEARS

Thanks to the creative team:
Senior Editor: Alice Peebles
Consultant: John Haywood
Fact Checking: Tom Jackson
Designer: Lauren Woods and collaborate agency

Hungry Tomato®
A division of Lerner Publishing Group, Inc.
241 First Avenue North
Minneapolis, MN 55401 USA

For reading levels and more information, look up
this title at www.lernerbooks.com.

Main body text set in Avenir Next Medium 10/12.
Typeface provided by Linotype AG.

Library of Congress Cataloging-in-Publication Data

The Cataloging-in-Publication Data for *The Modern World: The Last
Hundred Years* is on file at the Library of Congress.
ISBN 978-1-5124-5974-6 (lib. bdg.)
ISBN 978-1-5124-9876-9 (eb pdf)

Manufactured in the United States of America
1-43033-27702-10/13/2017

THE
MODERN
WORLD
THE LAST HUNDRED YEARS

by John Farndon
Illustrated by Christian Cornia

HUNGRY TOMATO®

Minneapolis

CONTENTS

The Last Hundred Years 6

New Century
1900-1910 9

The Great War
1910-1919 11

The Roaring Twenties
1920-1930 13

Depression Years
1930-1938 15

World War II
1939-1945 17

Cold War
1945-1956 19

The Space Age
1956-1966 20

Changing World
1967-1980 23

The Iron Curtain Drops
1980-1989 25

Millennium's End
1990-2000 27

Who's Who 28
Well, I Never 30
Index 32

North America

This was the USA's century. It became the world's richest country and a global superpower. The new American lifestyle—with its big cars and movies, giant refrigerators and home appliances—was the envy of the world.

South America

In Central and South America, many countries had to overcome cruel dictators and violent revolutions and deal with extreme poverty.

THE LAST HUNDRED YEARS

The twentieth century is the most recent time in our history. Cities grew massively, and amazing new technologies appeared: TV, computers, the car, and air travel. But many, many millions of people died in the two worst wars ever and in famines on a horrific scale.

Battle Key

★ On the maps, major battles are shown by this symbol.

Asia

By the end of the century, China and India were home to almost half the people in the world. The British left India and the French left Indochina in such chaos that wars erupted. But gradually, countries like South Korea and Japan emerged as dynamic centers of new technology.

Europe

Twice in the first half of the century, Europe was devastated by wars. But it was rebuilt and prospered after World War II. Social welfare systems reduced the poverty that once fueled conflict. For a while, Europe stayed sharply divided between West and East. But in time, even that division healed.

Eurasia

As old empires fell apart, Eurasia was left in a bit of a mess with plenty of conflict. But the discovery of oil made countries such as Saudi Arabia, Kuwait, and the United Arab Emirates very rich, and luxury shopping malls appeared in the desert.

Africa

At the start of the century, most of Africa was claimed by European countries as their own. Gradually, though, every African country won independence. But the divisions that had been created led to terrible conflicts, and disruption to traditional lifestyles meant countless African people suffered from disease, drought, and famine.

Australia

Australia and New Zealand became nations in their own right, separate from the UK. But they stayed part of the British Commonwealth, and huge numbers of their soldiers (called ANZACs) fought with Britain in both world wars.

Tough kids
1907 UK

When British army officer Baden-Powell came back from fighting Boer guerrillas in South Africa, he set up the Boy Scouts to help boys (and later, girls) learn how to be tough and independent.

Across Siberia
1904 Russia

In 1904, the Trans-Siberian Railway was completed. It is the world's longest railway line, running across Siberia a quarter of the way around the world, from Moscow to Vladivostok.

Moscow

PRUSSIA

Vladivostok

Forbidden City, Beijing

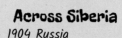

Kaiser Bill
1888–1918 Germany

German emperor Kaiser Wilhelm II was determined Germany would be top nation in Europe. He built a navy to rival Britain's and eventually drove Germany to war.

SOUTH AFRICA

The last emperor
1908–1912 China

Little Pu-Yi was only two years old when he became the last emperor of China and just six when he was removed by a revolution in 1912. He returned to power for just a few months in 1917.

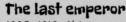

1901	1901	1901	1903	1904	1904
Australia unified	Marconi radios across the Atlantic	Death of Queen Victoria	Wright brothers' first flight	Russo-Japanese war begins	Trans-Siberian Railway finished

teddy's bear
1902 USA

On a bear hunt, gamekeepers tied a bear up for US president Teddy Roosevelt to shoot. Roosevelt refused, thinking it unfair. To mark the event, toymakers made a stuffed toy, the first teddy bear...........................

Takeoff!
1903 USA

On December 17, 1903, the Wright brothers, Orville and Wilbur, made history in Kitty Hawk, North Carolina, as Wilbur took off in their "Flyer" for the first-ever aircraft flight under power and control.

Kitty Hawk

NEW CENTURY
1900–1910

The twentieth century arrived with the first airplane flight, the first mass-produced cars, and the first radio broadcasts. But there were major tensions as Germany and Britain vied to be top dog. And the old Turkish and Russian empires were shaken by revolutions.

1905	1905	1906	1908	1908	1910
Revolution in Russia	Einstein's Theory of Special Relativity	San Francisco earthquake	Ford's Model T car mass-produced	Young Turk revolution in Ottoman Empire	Mexican Revolution

Votes for women
1912 UK

In 1912, women in the UK were not allowed to vote. So women called suffragettes protested by chaining themselves to railings and in many other ways. They won their battle in 1918.

Digging in
1914–1918 France

The German advance was soon halted in northeast France. For the rest of the war, the Germans faced the French and British from trenches dug in the mud, launching sporadic attacks. Millions of soldiers on both sides died from attacks and disease.

★ Ypres
★ the Somme
● Paris
★ Verdun
★ the Marne
Western Front

Over the top
1916 France

Sometimes soldiers were sent "over the top" (out of the trench) to attack opposing trenches. In 1916, this led to the appalling Battle of the Somme in which a million men were wounded or killed in just four months.

Peace at last
1918 France

German submarine attacks on ships made the USA so angry, it declared war on Germany in 1917. The next year, Germany was defeated and forced to sign an armistice (peace treaty) at 11 a.m. on November 11, 1918.

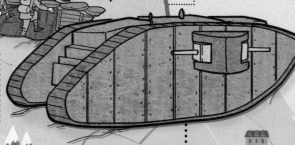

Moving castles
1916 France

Tanks were invented to launch attacks. They had heavy metal armor and metal tracks around the wheels to move across the muddy battlefield.

1910	**1912**	**1912**	**1914**	**1914**	**1914**
Japan takes over Korea	Chinese Empire replaced by a republic	Sinking of the *Titanic*	Franz Ferdinand assassinated	World War I begins	Russia defeated at Tannenberg

Russian Revolution
1917 Russia

The Russian people had had it with tsars—and the war was the last straw! So a revolutionary communist group called Bolsheviks took over the government in St. Petersburg and drove the tsar out. The tsar and his family were later executed.

THE GREAT WAR
1910–1919

In the early 1900s, Europe was waiting to explode. And in 1914, as countries threatened each other, the German army swept across Belgium and into France. So began the most terrible war the world had ever seen, World War I.

★ **Tannenberg**

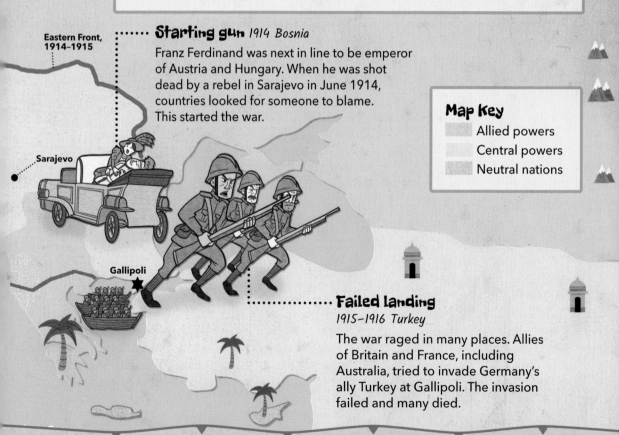

Eastern Front, 1914–1915

Starting gun *1914 Bosnia*

Franz Ferdinand was next in line to be emperor of Austria and Hungary. When he was shot dead by a rebel in Sarajevo in June 1914, countries looked for someone to blame. This started the war.

Sarajevo

Map Key

Allied powers
Central powers
Neutral nations

★ **Gallipoli**

Failed landing
1915–1916 Turkey

The war raged in many places. Allies of Britain and France, including Australia, tried to invade Germany's ally Turkey at Gallipoli. The invasion failed and many died.

1916	**1916**	**1917**	**1917**	**1918**	**1919**
Easter Rising in Ireland	Battle of the Somme	Russian Revolution	USA joins the war	Armistice ends World War I	Treaty of Versailles reorganizes Europe

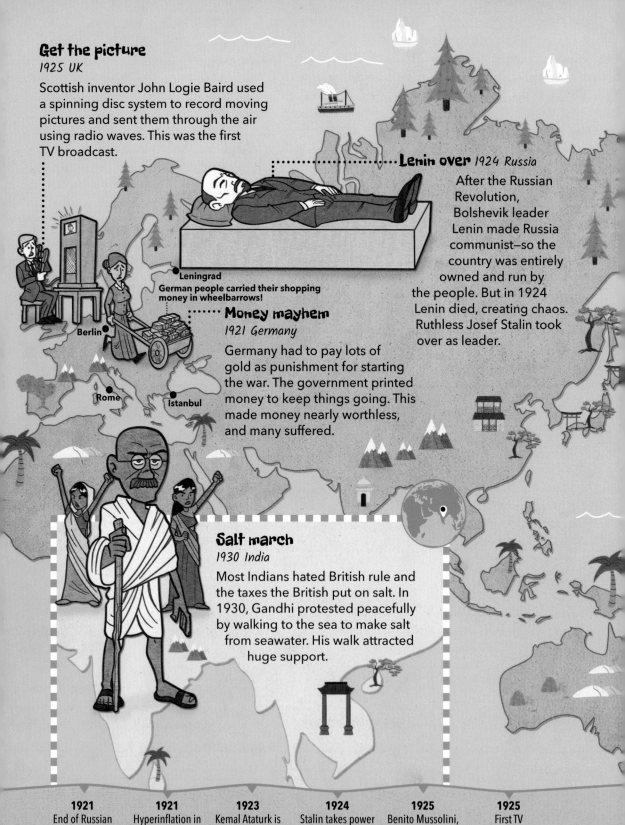

Get the picture
1925 UK
Scottish inventor John Logie Baird used a spinning disc system to record moving pictures and sent them through the air using radio waves. This was the first TV broadcast.

Lenin over 1924 Russia
After the Russian Revolution, Bolshevik leader Lenin made Russia communist—so the country was entirely owned and run by the people. But in 1924 Lenin died, creating chaos. Ruthless Josef Stalin took over as leader.

Leningrad
German people carried their shopping money in wheelbarrows!

Money mayhem
1921 Germany
Germany had to pay lots of gold as punishment for starting the war. The government printed money to keep things going. This made money nearly worthless, and many suffered.

Berlin

Rome

Istanbul

Salt march
1930 India
Most Indians hated British rule and the taxes the British put on salt. In 1930, Gandhi protested peacefully by walking to the sea to make salt from seawater. His walk attracted huge support.

1921	1921	1923	1924	1925	1925
End of Russian Civil War	Hyperinflation in Germany	Kemal Ataturk is Turkish president	Stalin takes power after Lenin's death	Benito Mussolini, dictator in Italy	First TV broadcast

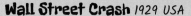

Wall Street Crash *1929 USA*

Millions of ordinary Americans borrowed money to invest in the stock market (shares in businesses) on New York's Wall Street. But in 1929, prices collapsed and all those people lost their money, starting the economic disaster called the Great Depression.

Free Soup for the Unemployed

Chicago●

●New York

Let's talk
1927 USA

The first films had no sound, except live musicians playing in the cinema. But in 1927, they made the first talkie, or movie with sound—*The Jazz Singer*.

AL JOLSON
THE JAZZ SINGER

THE ROARING TWENTIES
1920–1930

After the horrors of World War I, life in the big cities went wild, especially in the USA. Rich people partied. Industries boomed, and people were excited by modern things—cars, TV, talking movies, refrigerators—but the world was heading for trouble again.

1926	**1927**	**1927**	**1928**	**1929**	**1929**
General Strike of workers in Britain	Australian government in Canberra	*The Jazz Singer*, the first "talkie"	Penicillin discovered; bubble gum invented	St. Valentine's Day gangster massacre, Chicago	Wall Sreet Crash

German storm
1933–1945 Germany

After Adolf Hitler became the leader of Germany in 1933, his Nazi Party took total control of the country for their own terrible ends. People swore obedience at huge rallies and protest was dealt with mercilessly. Jews, Roma, and others were persecuted.

Leningrad

London

Madrid

Rome

Sky high
1931 USA

For 40 years after it was finished in 1931, the Empire State Building in New York was the world's tallest building at 1,454 ft. (443.2 m). It was a powerful symbol that America had arrived!

New York

Chicago gangster
1920–1933 USA

To stop people from drinking so much, the US government banned alcohol. In this time of Prohibition, gangsters sold drink illegally, especially in Chicago. The most infamous gangster was Al "Scarface" Capone.

Spanish tragedy
1936–1939 Spain

In Spain, a civil war began when the army under General Franco (Nationalists) toppled the elected government (Republicans), whom they thought were too liberal. Franco won and became dictator for 30 years.

1930	1931	1932	1933	1933	1933
First soccer World Cup	South Africa independent	Holodomor (man-made famine), Ukraine	Hitler becomes German chancellor	Roosevelt becomes US president	New Deal begins in USA

SOVIET UNION/ USSR (Russia and adjoining communist countries)

DEPRESSION YEARS
1930–1938

There was widepsread poverty and suffering as economic depression hit the world. In the USA, President Franklin D. Roosevelt's New Deal of government spending helped save the day. But in Germany, the Nazis came to power.

Russian hammer
1924–1953 USSR

Stalin took control in the Soviet Union, or USSR. Anyone protesting was arrested and shot or sent to Gulag prison camps. As he "modernized" farming, millions died of hunger between 1932–1933.

Istanbul

Beijing

Marching on
1934–1935 China

There was civil war in China. The communist Red Army escaped the Nationalist armies of Chiang Kai-shek with a Long March through the mountains, led in part by Mao Zedong.

Africa lion
1916–1974 Ethiopia

Haile Selassie was emperor of Abyssinia when it was attacked by Mussolini's fascist Italy. He was restored to power by the British and French and was thought of as the messiah by Rastafaris.

The Great Depression
1929–1939 Worldwide

For about 10 years after the Wall Street Crash, the world was gripped by the worst-ever economic slowdown. Tens of millions of people lost jobs and homes and faced starvation.

1934	1935	1936	1937	1938	1939
Mao Zedong begins Long March	Italy takes over Abyssinia	Spanish Civil War begins	Japan invades China	Germany takes over Czechoslovakia	Franco becomes Spanish dictator

Battle of Britain
1940 Britain

Germany quickly took over France, then targeted Britain with waves of attacks by bomber planes. But small British fighter planes (Hurricanes and Spitfires) held them off.

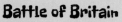

The Bulge, 1944

Siege of Leningrad, 1941-1944

D-Day landings, 1944

Anzio, 1944

Monte Cassino, 1944

Holocaust
1939–1945 Germany

After the war, the Allied armies reached the death camps, such as Auschwitz in Poland, where the Nazis had taken millions of people, mostly Jews, to starve or be gassed to death.

Stalingrad, 1942-1943

D-Day
1944 France

The Allies' response in Western Europe began on June 6, 1944, when they landed a huge army on the coast of Normandy. The day for the invasion was code-named D-Day.

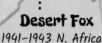

Desert Fox
1941–1943 N. Africa

As European colonies in North Africa were drawn into the war, fierce tank battles raged across the desert. Germany's brilliant tank commander was Erwin Rommel, the "Desert Fox."

Singapore, 1942

1939	1940	1940	1941	1941	1942
Nazis invade Poland	Nazis invade France, Netherlands	Battle of Britain	Nazis invade the Soviet Union	Japan attacks Pearl Harbor	Main phase of the Holocaust begins

WORLD WAR II
1939–1945

In 1939, Nazi Germany invaded Poland. In protest, Britain and France declared war on Germany. The whole world was soon dragged into a terrible six-year war that killed up to 85 million people, with the Axis powers (Germany, Italy, and Japan) on one side and the Allied Forces on the other.

Russian Front
1942–1943 USSR

The USSR suffered terrible losses in the war, with over 11 million soldiers killed. It won the Battle of Stalingrad (now Volgograd), but two million people were killed or wounded in the city streets.

Pearl Harbor
1941 Hawaii, Pacific

At first, the USA kept out of the war. Then, in 1941, Japanese aircraft attacked the US Navy at Pearl Harbor, killing 2,500 and sinking five ships. The USA joined the war at once.

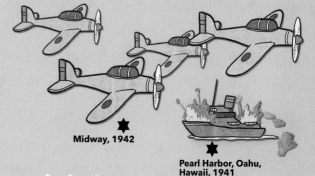

Midway, 1942

Pearl Harbor, Oahu, Hawaii, 1941

Iwo Jima, 1945

Hiroshima hell
1945 Japan

To attempt to end the war quickly, the USA dropped atom bombs on two Japanese cities—Hiroshima and Nagasaki—with devastating effects, killing 129,000 people. Nuclear weapons have never been used since.

Bataan, 1942

Map Key
▮ under Axis control
▮ under Allied control

1942	1942	1944	1945	1945	1945
US victory at the Battle of Midway	Battle of Stalingrad begins	Allied D-Day landings in France	VE day: Allies win the war in Europe	Hiroshima and Nagasaki bombed	Yalta Conference ends the war

Iron Curtain
1945–1991 Europe

Europe was split by a border so hard to cross that it was called the Iron Curtain. To the east, countries were controlled by the USSR, and people couldn't leave without permission.

The tops!
1953 Nepal

New Zealand's Edmund Hillary and his Nepalese guide, or sherpa, Tenzing Norgay were the first to climb the world's highest mountain, Mt. Everest.

Capitalism vs. Communism
1945–onwards

In capitalism, everything is run by buying and selling things. In communism, the community owns everything and distributes things fairly. In the USSR, tragically, many civilians died as Stalin's government tried to make their version of communism work.

WEST GERMANY

EAST GERMANY

Moscow

West Pakistan

Mt. Everest

INDIA

East Pakistan

CHINA

TAIWAN

Indian split
1947 India and Pakistan

When the British left India, they split it between mainly Hindu India and mainly Muslim Pakistan. But some Muslims were trapped in India and Hindus in Pakistan, which triggered a terrible civil war.

Health for all
1948 UK

To avoid the social problems that led to war, many European countries set up welfare systems to look after people. In the UK, the National Health Service made medical treatment free for all.

1945	1945	1947	1948	1949	1949
Korea split into North and South	United Nations founded	India and Pakistan independent	Murder of Gandhi	Split of Germany into East and West	Mao takes control of China

Red China
1949 China

After a civil war, the Red Army, led by Mao Zedong, took control of China. Mao turned China into a communist country. Landlords were executed and land redistributed to the poor.

Aid for Europe
1948–1952 USA

To rebuild Western Europe after the war, and slow the spread of communism, US secretary of state George Marshall launched a plan for the USA to pump in a lot of money.

New York

COLD WAR
1945–1956

Despite their victory, the Allies were divided. The USA believed capitalism was the only way to go. The USSR (Soviet Union) thought the same about communism. Europe was split down the middle, as a "Cold War" (a war of words and threats) developed between the USA and the USSR.

Argentina for Eva
1952 Argentina

Poor country girl turned actress Eva Duarte married Colonel Juan Perón. When Perón was elected president of Argentina, Eva became a champion of working people. She was very popular, but died aged just 33.

ARGENTINA
Buenos Aires

Map Key
■ Communist countries
■ Countries aligned with the USA

1950	1951	1952	1953	1953	1956
Korean War begins	Paris Treaty starts EU first steps	Eva Perón dies in Argentina	Stalin dies	Hillary and Norgay climb Mt. Everest	Hungarians rebel

President down
1963 USA

In 1962, US president John F. Kennedy and Russian leader Khrushchev just avoided a nuclear war over Russian missiles in Cuba. The next year, Kennedy was shot dead in Dallas, Texas.

Elvis shakes
1956–1958 USA

Elvis Presley was the first pop superstar. His superstyled look and his mix of country music with rock 'n' roll and blues had every teenager dancing and girls screaming in delight.

Dallas, Texas

CUBA

Revolution in Cuba 1959 Cuba

Cuban dictator Batista was overthrown in a revolution led by Fidel Castro and Argentine Che Guevara. Castro made Cuba communist. Guevara became a hero for rebels.

THE SPACE AGE
1956–1966

The space age began when the USSR launched the first satellite in 1957. But rivalry between the USSR and USA in building nuclear arms brought near disaster. Meanwhile, Mao's policies caused many Chinese to die of hunger. But pop music made people smile and dance.

1957	**1958**	**1959**	**1961**	**1961**	**1962**
USSR launches Sputnik 1	Famine in China	Cuban Revolution	Berlin Wall built	First human in space	Cuban Missile Crisis

Beatlemania
1963–1970 UK and USA

Liverpool band The Beatles were the first pop sensation, famous for "moptop" haircuts and sharp suits. Girls got super excited and mobbed them when they appeared in public. It was called Beatlemania.

Liverpool

West Berlin

WEST GERMANY (FDR)

EAST GERMANY (GDR)

Spaceman
1961 space

Russian cosmonaut Yuri Gagarin became the first human in space, when his *Vostok 1* spacecraft circled Earth on April 12, 1961.

Great Leap Forward 1958 China

Chinese leader Mao handed over all farmland to giant communes and forced farmworkers to make steel. It was a catastrophe—55 million people died of starvation.

Beijing

Walled off 1961 Berlin

West Berlin was a tiny bit of West Germany (FDR) locked inside East Germany (GDR). In 1961, the GDR built the Berlin Wall to stop East Germans getting to West Berlin.

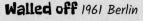

1962	1962	1963	1963	1964	1966
Algeria gains independence	The Beatles' first record	Martin Luther King's "I Have a Dream" speech	Assassination of John F. Kennedy	Racial segregation ends in the USA	China's Cultural Revolution begins

Irish troubles *1969–1997 Northern Ireland*

Northern Ireland was troubled by terrorist bombs and killings. Nationalists, who want Northern Ireland to join the Irish Republic, struggled against Unionists, who wanted to stay united to Britain.

Northern Ireland

Mao and Deng

1966–1976 China

Mao thought culture threatened communism. He launched a Cultural Revolution and a Red Guard of young people to persecute intellectuals and destroy books and historic relics. In 1976, Mao died and was replaced by Deng Xiaoping.

Beijing

Tehran, focus of Iran's 1979 Muslim revolution

North Vietnam

Paris protests

1968 France

Students, poets, and musicians joined workers to protest on the streets against a world run for the rich. President de Gaulle's government survived the crisis, but France was changed.

South Vietnam

Vietnam War *1955–1975 Vietnam*

After the French left, Vietnam split in two. The communist North urged Viet Cong guerrillas to fight in the jungles of the South to reunite the country. The US intervened to stop a communist takeover. But after a bitter war, the US withdrew and Vietnam was reunited.

1968	**1968**	**1969**	**1969**	**1971**	**1972**
Assassination of Martin Luther King	Prague Spring changes; Paris protests	Troubles begin in Northern Ireland	Men land on the moon	Bangladesh independence	Bloody Sunday in Northern Ireland

Summer of Love *1967 USA*

Young people wore robes and flowers and grew their hair long to protest against the Vietnam War and a world ruled by money. These "hippies" converged on San Francisco to celebrate peace, love, and rock music. ···········

San Francisco

CHANGING WORLD
1967-1980

In this time of trouble and change, young people in the West protested and went to rock festivals to dream of a better world. In Asia, there was terrible suffering in Vietnam and Cambodia and in China's Cultural Revolution.

Scorched Somozas *1979 Nicaragua* ···········

NICARAGUA

For a long while, Nicaragua was ruled by the American-backed dictators of the Somoza family. But in 1979, the Somozas were overthrown by the Sandinista rebels, who championed poor people's rights.

On the moon
1969 the moon

The US *Apollo 11* spacecraft made the first manned voyage to land on the moon. On July 20, 1969, astronauts Neil Armstrong and Buzz Aldrin were the first humans to set foot on the moon.

1973	**1973**	**1975**	**1975-1979**	**1976**	**1979**
Military takeover in Chile	Watergate scandal in Washington	Vietnam War ends	Mass murders in Cambodia's Killing Fields	Death of Mao Zedong	Iranian Revolution

Solidarity! *1980–1989 Poland*

Workers in Poland's Gdańsk shipyards, led by Lech Wałęsa, formed the union Solidarity. Soviet bosses tried to crush them, but they battled on and Solidarity were elected to lead the Polish government.

USSR

● Moscow

Gorby's reforms
1985–1991 USSR

As Soviet leader, Gorbachev led reforms called *glasnost* (openness) and *perestroika* (remaking) to give more freedom. But people wanted much more freedom, and the USSR soon broke up.

Rising Sun *1926–1989 Japan*

Shōwa (Hirohito) died in 1989, after 62 years as emperor of Japan. Japan was badly beaten in the war, and Shōwa was a symbol of its amazing economic recovery.

JAPAN

Wall's end
1989 Germany

As Hungary and Poland rebelled, East German authorities realized the Berlin Wall was not working. They opened the gates to let people walk through, and soon it was torn down altogether.

1980	1980	1980	1982	1982	1984
Zimbabwe independence recognized	Iran-Iraq War begins	Ronald Reagan elected US president	Falklands War	First CD players	Miners' strike in the UK

Acting president
1981–1989 USA

When film actor Ronald Reagan became fortieth US president, some said he'd be a flop. But his friendly meetings with Soviet leader Gorbachev may have helped to end the Cold War.

Washington, D.C.

THE IRON CURTAIN DROPS
1980–1989

The mighty Soviet Union was cracking and the Cold War was melting. First, Polish shipyard workers demanded more control. Then, Soviet leader Mikhail Gorbachev and US president Reagan agreed to halt the nuclear arms race. And in 1989, communist countries in Europe rebelled.

NICARAGUA

Iran guns
1979–1990 Nicaragua

The Contra rebels fought to bring down the Nicaraguan government. They were secretly funded by the US military by sales of arms to Iran, a scandal called the Iran-Contra affair.

Falklands War
1982 Falkland Islands/Malvinas

The Falkland Islands in the South Atlantic are British. But Argentine dictator Galtieri claimed them for Argentina. In 1982, he sent an army to invade. The British fought back and drove the Argentines off the islands again.

ARGENTINA

Falkland Is.

1985	1985	1988	1989	1989	1989
Live Aid concerts help famine victims in Ethiopia	Gorbachev is Soviet leader	Pinochet's rule in Chile ends	Berlin Wall comes down	Tiananmen Square massacre in China	Exxon Valdez oil spill, Alaska

Dolly the sheep
1996 UK
Dolly the sheep was the first mammal cloned from ordinary body cells. This means Dolly had only one parent, not two. Scientists took the cells from one sheep and inserted them into another's egg to grow and be born.

ESTONIA
LATVIA
LITHUANIA

UKRAINE

Bug date 2000
Some experts said all computers would crash when the year 2000 came up. They called it the Y2K, or Millennium Bug. Nothing happened . . .

The global net 1990 Switzerland
Scientist Tim Berners-Lee changed the world when he invented the World Wide Web. The WWW allowed computers to link to files on other computers around the world via the Internet.

Drug wars
1993 Colombia
Colombian drug barons like Pablo Escobar got mega-rich selling illegal drugs in the USA. Escobar was murdered in 1993. Others took his place, but the Columbian government began to win the battle against them.

45632

South African freedom
1994 South Africa
Nelson Mandela was held in jail for 27 years for protesting against apartheid, the racist system in South Africa. In 1990, he was freed to negotiate an end to apartheid. Four years later, apartheid was over and Mandela was the country's first black president.

SOUTH
AFRICA

Cape Town ●

1990	1990	1991	1992	1993	1993
World Wide Web invented	Gulf War begins	Breakup of Soviet Union	European Union begins	Military rule ends in South Korea	Slovakia and Czech Republic split

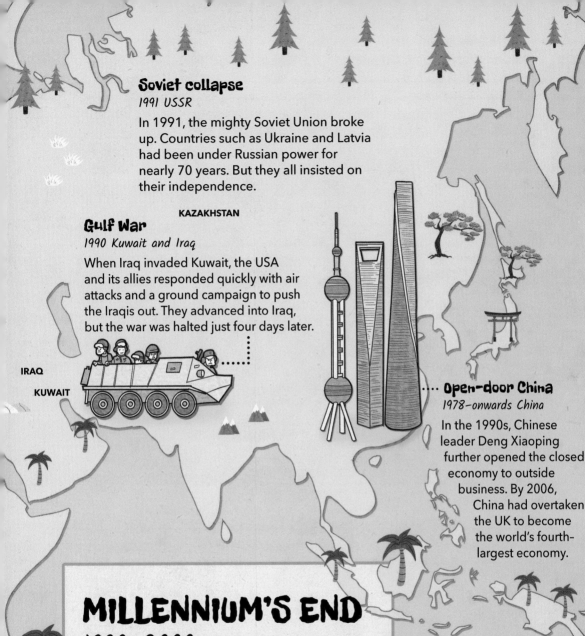

Soviet collapse
1991 USSR

In 1991, the mighty Soviet Union broke up. Countries such as Ukraine and Latvia had been under Russian power for nearly 70 years. But they all insisted on their independence.

KAZAKHSTAN

Gulf War
1990 Kuwait and Iraq

When Iraq invaded Kuwait, the USA and its allies responded quickly with air attacks and a ground campaign to push the Iraqis out. They advanced into Iraq, but the war was halted just four days later.

IRAQ

KUWAIT

Open-door China
1978-onwards China

In the 1990s, Chinese leader Deng Xiaoping further opened the closed economy to outside business. By 2006, China had overtaken the UK to become the world's fourth-largest economy.

MILLENNIUM'S END
1990-2000

The decade began well. The Internet arrived with the invention of the World Wide Web. The Soviet Union broke up. European nations joined the European Union. Some people thought the world's problems were coming to an end. They were wrong . . .

1994	**1994**	**1995**	**1997**	**1998**	**1999**
Apartheid officially ends in South Africa	Genocide in Rwanda	Bosnian War	Hong Kong returns to China	Good Friday Agreement in Northern Ireland	Hugo Chavez elected in Venezuela

WHO'S WHO

The twentieth century was a time of conflict, and in this book you have met groups of countries that fought wars, such as the Axis and Allies, and groups involved in political strife, such as the Sandinistas.

1903

Nicaraguan rebels: Sandinistas

1961–present

The Sandinistas are a democratic socialist party in Nicaragua. They took their name from a rebel hero of the 1920s, Augusto Sandino, and overthrew the dictator Somoza in 1979.

Big brothers: Bolsheviks

1903–1922

In 1903, the main Russian protest group split in two: the Bolsheviks (biggest part) and the Mensheviks (smallest part). The Bolsheviks, led by Lenin, were the more extreme and took over the Revolution after 1917.

Red destroyers: Red Guard

1966–1968

The Red Guard were young Chinese people recruited by Mao Zedong for his Cultural Revolution. Their task was to attack the "four olds": old customs, old culture, old habits, and old ideas. They destroyed art, books, and museums and persecuted teachers.

Vietnamese rebels: Viet Cong

1954–1976

When Vietnam was split in two in 1954, the Viet Cong were a rebel group that formed in the South to fight against the split. They fought a guerrilla war against the USA in the Vietnam War.

Nastiest ever: Nazis
1920–1945

The Nazis were the extreme party that controlled Germany in the 1930s. They imposed their nationalism and terrible racist ideas on all and drove the mass killing of Jews and others.

One Ireland: Irish nationalists
1921–present

Irish nationalists or republicans believe it was wrong to separate Northern Ireland from the rest of Ireland in 1920. They struggle to reunite them.

Fighting together: Allies
1939–1945

The Allies were 26 nations that joined to fight Germany and the Axis powers in World War II. They included Britain, France, Poland, Australia, Canada, India, the Soviet Union, and the USA.

Two Irelands: Irish unionists
1921–present

Unionists think Northern Ireland should remain part of the United Kingdom, separate from the rest of Ireland.

Fighting together: Axis
1940–1945

The Axis powers were the countries that fought the Allies in World War II: Germany, Italy, and Japan. They were linked by what was called the Berlin-Rome-Tokyo Axis.

Red menace: Khmer Rouge
1968–1979

The Khmer Rouge were an offshoot of the Vietnamese communists who took over Cambodia. Under their leader Pol Pot, they murdered many people on farms, an event known as the Killing Fields.

2000

WELL, I NEVER . . .

Some strange stories from the last century:

DON'T SHOOT, IT'S CHRISTMAS! ············

In places along the front in World War I, German and English soldiers decided to call a halt to the fighting for Christmas in 1914. On Christmas Eve in one place, the story is told that soldiers from each side started singing Christmas songs across the battlefield and some even climbed out of the trenches and had a game of soccer.

LIGHTS ON

The German city of Konstanz escaped bombing in World War II with a trick. It was quite close to the border with neutral Switzerland. So the city left all its lights full on and fooled enemy bombers into thinking it must be in Switzerland.

IS THE WAR OVER? ············

After Japan surrendered at the end of World War II in 1945, a handful of Japanese soldiers in remote parts of the Philippines and other islands never heard about it—or chose to ignore it. Called holdouts, they continued to stay in hiding for more than 30 years.

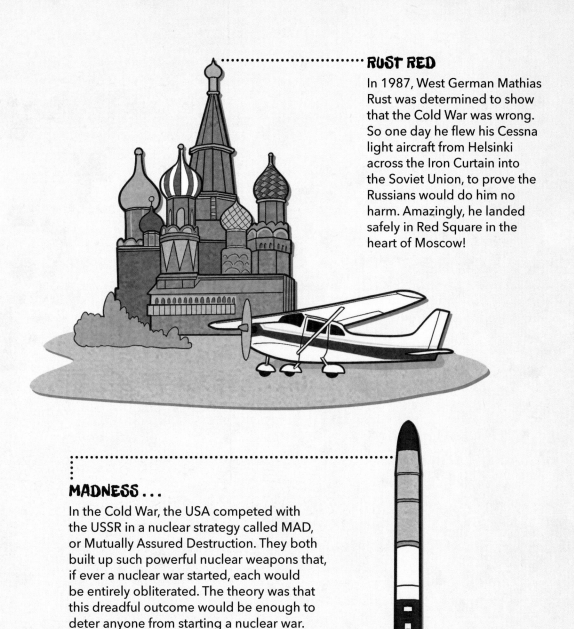

RUST RED

In 1987, West German Mathias Rust was determined to show that the Cold War was wrong. So one day he flew his Cessna light aircraft from Helsinki across the Iron Curtain into the Soviet Union, to prove the Russians would do him no harm. Amazingly, he landed safely in Red Square in the heart of Moscow!

MADNESS . . .

In the Cold War, the USA competed with the USSR in a nuclear strategy called MAD, or Mutually Assured Destruction. They both built up such powerful nuclear weapons that, if ever a nuclear war started, each would be entirely obliterated. The theory was that this dreadful outcome would be enough to deter anyone from starting a nuclear war. Fortunately, no one tested it out.

INDEX

Africa, 7, 15, 27
atom bomb, 17
Australia, 7, 11, 29

Berlin Wall, 21, 24

China, 8, 15, 19, 21-22,
    27-28
Cold War, 19, 31
Cuban Revolution, 20

Dolly the sheep, 26
drug wars, 26

Empire State Building, 14

Falklands War, 25
first flight, 9
France, 16-17, 22, 29

Gandhi, 12
gangsters, 14
Germany, 8, 12, 21, 24
Great Depression, 15

hippies, 23
holocaust, 16-17

India, 12, 18
Iron Curtain, 18, 24-25

Japan, 17, 24, 29

Kennedy, John F., 20

Mandela, Nelson, 26-27
Mao Zedong, 15, 19-22,
    28
Marshall Plan, 19
moon landing, 23

National Health Service,
    18
Nazis, 14, 29
Nicaragua, 23, 25, 28
Northern Ireland, 22, 29

Pearl Harbor, 17
Perón, Eva, 19
pop superstars, 20-21

Russian Revolution,
    11-12, 28

Selassie, Haile, 15
Solidarity, 24
space exploration, 20-21,
    23
Spanish Civil War, 14
suffragettes, 10

talkies, 13
teddy bears, 9
television, 12
Trans-Siberian railway, 8

USA, 6, 9, 13-15, 17,
    19-20, 23, 25
USSR (Soviet Union),
    12, 15-16, 18-20, 24,
    27-28

Vietnam War, 22, 28-29

Wall Street Crash, 13
Wilhelm II, Kaiser, 8
World War I, 10-11
World War II, 16-17, 29
World Wide Web, 27

The Author

John Farndon is Royal Literary Fellow at City&Guilds in London, UK, and the author of a huge number of books for adults and children on science, technology and history, including international bestsellers. He has been shortlisted six times for the Royal Society's Young People's Book Prize.

The Illustrator

Italian-born Christian Cornia decided at the age of four to be a comic-book artist, and is essentially self-taught. He has illustrated Marvel Comics and is one of the artists for the Scooby-Doo character in Italy and the USA. He also teaches animation at the Scuola Internazionale di Comics in Italy.